My Pet

My Parakeet

By Pamela Walker

Welcome Books

Children's Press
A Division of Grolier Publishing
New York / London / Hong Kong / Sydney
Danbury, Connecticut

Photo Credits: Cover, pp. 5, 7, 9, 11, 13, 15, 17, 19, 21 by Maura Boruchow
Contributing Editor: Jeri Cipriano
Book Design: Nelson Sa

Visit Children's Press on the Internet at:
http://publishing.grolier.com

Library of Congress Cataloging-in-Publication Data

Walker, Pamela, 1958-
  My parakeet / by Pamela Walker.
    p. cm.—(My pet)
  Includes bibliographical references and index.
  ISBN 0-516-23187-1 (lib. bdg.)—ISBN 0-516-23290-8 (pbk.)
    1. Budgerigar—Juvenile literature. [1. Parakeets. 2. Pets.] I. Title. II. My pet (Children's
Press)

  SF473.B8 W36 2000
  636.6′864—dc21

                                                                00-031634

Contents

1 Meet Pop   4

2 Pop Sings   8

3 Pop Talks   10

4 Feeding Pop   12

5 New Words   22

6 To Find Out More   23

7 Index   24

8 About the Author   24

Hi, I'm Joe.

This is my **parakeet**, Pop.

Pop lives in a cage.

Pop sits on a **perch**.

7

Pop swings.

Pop sings, too!

9

Pop talks.

Pop can say words.

Pop can say, "Hi, Joe!" and "Bye, Joe!"

Every day I feed Pop.

I give Pop parakeet food.

13

Pop needs other kinds of food, too.

I feed Pop lettuce.

I feed Pop bits of carrot.

15

Pop has many toys.

Pop has **hoops**.

Pop has a bell.

Pop hops on my finger.

I stroke Pop's feathers.

19

At night, I cover the cage.

Pop is quiet.

Goodnight, Pop!

New Words

hoops rings
parakeet a small bird
  with bright feathers
perch bar that birds
  sit on

To Find Out More

Books

How to Hide a Parakeet & Other Birds
by Ruth Heller
Grosset & Dunlap

Pete the Parakeet
by Sharon Gordon and Paul Harvey
Troll Communications

Web Site

Me & My Budgie
http://www.budgie.org
A budgie is another name for a parakeet.
On this site you can find out everything you
need to know about owning and caring
for a parakeet.

Index

cage, 6

carrot, 14

hoops, 16

lettuce, 14

parakeet, 4, 12

perch, 6

About the Author

Pamela Walker lives in Brooklyn, New York.

Reading Consultants

Kris Flynn, Coordinator, Small School District Literacy, The San Diego County Office of Education

Shelly Forys, Certified Reading Recovery Specialist, W.J. Zahnow Elementary School, Waterloo, IL

Peggy McNamara, Professor, Bank Street College of Education, Reading and Literacy Program